Odds

and

Ends

Stories, Questions, Reflections, and Challenges

Michelle Elliott

With love to my husband, my kids, and my very good friends who have loved, encouraged, and supported me, and still continue to do so in my journey. I love you all!

And in memory of my Mom
Debi Malone
February 28, 1949-October 16, 2022

Contents

Introduction

Inside are stories, questions, reflections, and challenges based on my own journey. The topics, thoughts, ideas, notions, and questions are an invitation into a very real, intimate view of my life, my world, and my inner landscape.

Each story stands alone and is presented as a sort of devotional...not in the traditional sense of the word...but as something to think about and consider, questions to ask yourself, and topics to share with those you love.

I hope to encourage connection and vulnerability... something a lot of us, myself included, struggle with. These stories can be used as a 31 day devotional, small group study, for your own personal use...really, you get to decide.

At the end of the day, I hope that through my stories, you feel like someone gets it and that you are not alone. I hope you feel heard, seen, valued, accepted, and loved. Some of my stories you may relate to, some you won't, and that's okay. The point is, in whatever circumstances we face, whether they are alike or different, we share the struggle.

Brick Project

1

Does That Look Straight To You?

One summer, I was placing some bricks in our back yard to partition a section I wanted to put mulch in, and eventually plant flowers. I carefully placed each brick in line with the one before it, making sure each one was level on the top and side, until I reached the end of the section.

The next morning, as my husband and I were looking through our kitchen window at my work, I asked him, "Does that look straight to you?"

Something about it didn't look quite right to me, but I couldn't identify what it was. My husband has an eye for detail and I trusted that he would see it if something was off. He thought for a minute and said, "It looks straight but to be sure, you have to measure the distance of each one from the house to make sure they are all the same distance."

That morning I got my tape measure and went to work. As I moved down the line, I noticed that each brick was off just a hair...that's Oklahoma speak for a small degree in distance...from the house, than the one before it. The degree was so slight, you wouldn't notice just by looking at it. As I had placed each brick, I had managed to place it out of alignment, ever so slightly, from the one before it. At the beginning of the row, it wasn't a big deal, however at the end, those "hairs" added up to be inches. What looked straight to me, wasn't.

Life is like that. My short term wants can get in the way of my long term goals and if I give in to my short term wants long enough, I will not reach my long term goals.

For instance if, over time, I impulsively spend money on that thing I just have to have *right now*, I may not be able to get the thing I've wanted for a long time that requires saving for. If I daily give in to the impulse to just grab whatever is quick to eat in the moment, I may not realize my long term goal of being healthy. If I want to get the house cleaned, spend time with family and friends, exercise, spend time with the dog, or do other things that are meaningful to me, and I spend all day on my phone playing games, the day will be gone and I'll be sad because I didn't do the things I really wanted to do. You get the idea.

The thing is, some of the time these things are okay. Done once in a while, or even twice or three times in a while :), they will not derail me. It's just part of being human and even is necessary to be able to live a life of freedom and choice. Done consistently over time, I can find myself going a completely different direction and not realize it.

As the house was the "true north" for the brick placement, I need to have something in place that will encourage me to keep checking in with myself asking, "will this lead me to where I want to be?" It will be easier for me then, to maintain the course over time and get where I want to be.

What are things that get in the way of where you want to be?

Do you have something in place to refer back to, to make sure you're still headed in the direction you want to be going?

2

A Lot of This!

Have you had moments, days, weeks, months, seasons, in life when it's just a lot? I know you have. So have I. Everyone has. I am in a season like that. Maybe you can relate!

In 2014, I had a car accident, the fault of the other driver, that totaled my car. I was lucky to have survived it.

In 2015, my husband learned he had hypertrophic obstructive cardiomyopathy...the condition where athletes, in seemingly perfect health, suddenly die. His heart wall was too thick, his valves were leaking, and we had no idea. I came home one day to find him in the kitchen, ghostly white, chilled, and feeling weak. We thought it was the flu.

We had a commitment we couldn't miss so we opted to divide and conquer. I went to the meeting, and he went to Urgent Care. I expected he would receive a prescription, then he'd be home. Hours later, I got a text from him saying they were sending him to the ER with heart issues. WHAT????!!!!! Heart issues???

We took a little trip to Mayo Clinic in Rochester for open heart surgery to remove a portion of his heart wall and repair the valves. We were lucky. Lots of people don't get advanced warning. He made a complete recovery and I am very grateful.

Between 2017 and 2023, my mom was diagnosed with lung cancer, I lost my best dog, Mom had a partial lung lobectomy, I lost my other dog, Mom developed a new cancer, this one more aggressive, and underwent a round of cyber-knife radiation, I lost my mother-in-law, two weeks later my grandpa, I lost a grandmother, and two weeks later, a cousin, I lost my other grandma and Mom underwent a third round of radiation..more cancer.

On October 16, 2022, I lost my mom.

So what do you do when there's a lot of this? When you feel like you can barely keep your head above water? When you cry more than you smile?

I have a support network of friends and family who help me see the good and not just the sad. I try to do things that bring me joy trusting that joy will come...if not in the moment, for sure later. I say no when I need to, and yes when I can. I let people "see" me as much as I can. I'm still working on being vulnerable! And, I lean on my faith.

I am still on the journey. Some days feel great, and some days feel sad. It's part of being human. I am embracing that in life, there are times of joy and there are times of pain. Without the pain, I wouldn't appreciate the joy!

Can you relate?

What helps you get through the hard things?

3

Chapters

A while back, I was reading and thought about chapters. What is a chapter? What's its purpose? According to prowritingaid.com each chapter builds a sequence in the framework of your story...it may transition the reader from one plot point toward the next. Hm. So what if I looked at life as a sequence of chapters, and what would those chapters look like?

We all have a narrative, a story, composed of all the things that went into making us who we are today, and what those events say to us about us.

My story has hard parts, sad parts I'd like to forget, happy parts, WHAT WAS I THINKING parts, parts I don't remember but there are pictures that tell a story, and parts that are yet to be.

How will I tell my story? Will I make it sad, not giving a voice to happy things? Will I make it happy, ignoring the hard and sad things? Or will I tell it in a way that embraces all the parts, and let it say something good about me?

I think I'll tell the whole story, and instead of imagining that it says something bad about me, I think I'll let it say something good. I'll celebrate the things I've learned from, triumphed over, healed from, happy things I've experienced, and even parts I feel ashamed of, because without them, I wouldn't be who I am today.

All the segments of my life add up to be a whole book full of ups, downs, twists, turns, unexpected plot changes, heartbreaks, happy times, sidetracks, full speed ahead moments, aha moments, quiet moments, and all the moments that are still to come.

What will you let your chapters say to you about you? I hope it's something good!

4

Do You See Her?

Luke 7:44 "Turning to the woman, he said to Simon, 'Do you see this woman? I entered your house; you gave me no water for my feet, but she, with her tears, has washed my feet and wiped them with her hair.'" The passage goes on to tell us all the ways she gave to him, that all her many sins were forgiven and that's why she loved much.

My take away: Jesus SAW her. Dr. Curt Thompson, a psychiatrist I follow says, "Our deepest desire as humans is to be known, to be seen, soothed, safe, and secure. It is foundational to developing a secure attachment."

Can you imagine what that felt like, to know that even at her worst, when she may have felt the most unlovable, unwanted, alone, and rejected, he saw her?

I want to experience what it feels like to be seen like that by the One who loves me most. My mind knows that he sees me, but sometimes my heart has trouble feeling it.

Do you feel known-seen, soothed, safe, and secure?

Or do you struggle sometimes like I do?

Off Center

5

Off Center

Our TV is mounted above our fireplace mantle, and on that mantle are two small reed diffuser bottles. They are empty, and I was trying to figure out what I would use them for. I decided to put some artificial flowers in them.

I finally found some I liked (I'm very picky) and was placing them in the bottles. From where I stood, on the right side of the TV as I was facing it, the distance between the corner of the TV, to the bottles, to the wall on each side, didn't look equal to me. It all looked off center.

I said to my husband, who was sitting on the couch directly in front of the TV, "These look off to me and I can't decide why." He said, "The one on the right is maybe an inch off but otherwise they look good." (He has an amazing eye for detail!) So I moved the bottle over an inch and moved to the front where he was sitting. And guess what? Everything looked balanced.

When I was looking at the setup from the side, my perception of balance was skewed and everything looked off center. When I moved to the front where I could see the whole scenario, everything was in balance.

So it is with situations, thoughts, and feelings I experience. If I am firmly entrenched in my own view, I will see a skewed picture. If I zoom out and look at it from a different vantage point, I can see the whole picture. And that looks WAY different!

I can get locked in to believing the way I see it is the way it is, the way I feel about it means it's true, and my perception of it is fact. What I'm realizing is, there's always a different perspective. It doesn't mean I'm wrong and something or someone else is right. It just means that there are other ways of seeing things that show a fuller picture of what I'm experiencing.

Ya know what though, it hurts my pride to admit that I might not have THE answer to everything and my perception may be only a partial lens to view through OUCH!

It's laughable almost. If I had held on to my perspective, I would have insisted that the TV and everything else was off center and would have wanted it moved. And, after all that effort, I would have seen that it was all centered to begin with and now it really IS off center!

Thoughts to think about!!

Are you able to take a step back and look at things from another perspective even if it's different than yours?

6

Jesus Owns The Space

A friend posted this on social media:

"Last night, a teenage girl brought a friend for the first time to a gathering we had in our home. We'll call her friend Kate. Kate is very confident, self-assured, knows what she wants. For fun, I asked with excitement if they both would like to see my prayer room. They lit up with smiles and said, 'Yes!' As they crawled in they started to ooh and aah, eyes wide.

I struck up a conversation with Kate about how she was God's idea and that Jesus is the blueprint and design of her life. As she was blushing and smiling, her friend said, 'Why are you acting so weird? You never act like this?' Kate replied, 'I know. Usually when I walk into a room, it's mine. It's my room.' She was implying that she owns the atmosphere where ever she goes. But then she paused, and with a look of astonishment and wonder said, 'But this...is not my room.'"

What followed was a conversation about the Lover of her soul and her desire to then and there get baptized in our bathtub. Unfortunately, her mother on the phone emphatically said 'No!' but sweet Kate encountered the love of Jesus. She walked into a room that was owned by him."

As I was reflecting, I realized that I can walk as if I don't have authority, what's out there is bigger than who's inside me, I don't have influence, or I'm invisible.

Jesus owns the space. He owns the air, the ground, the trees, the earth, everything in it, and he lives inside me. So wherever I go, he goes. He is light and everywhere I step, light shines and infiltrates darkness....shatters it.

What if I really lived that out? How would I see the world? How would my life change?

Do you walk in the confidence that Jesus owns the space?

If not, what would be different if you did?

7

Let Me Serve You

In church one Sunday as the pastor was talking, I "heard" Jesus say to me, "Let me serve you."

What?! You've got to be kidding me! How can I let you serve me?! I don't do a lot of things right. I sometimes don't know how to follow you or if I do know, my will gets in the way and I push against you. Seriously, what the heck!

I was reminded of John 13:8 (TPT). "Peter looked at Jesus and said, 'You'll never wash my dirty feet—never!'" I imagine Peter felt like I did. No way! You are holy, perfect, the embodiment of love, of life, of light, of all that is good, and I don't deserve for you to care for me in that way. How can I let you do that?

The rest of the verse says, "But Peter, if you don't allow me to wash your feet," Jesus responded, "then you will not be able to share life with me."

I want to share life with Jesus, be close to him, feel his nearness, and hear his words, but what does it look like for me to let him serve me? I don't even know. I can't understand it. Maybe that's the point.

I sometimes think I don't deserve it, but he wants to. He knows all about the things I would never tell another living soul if I didn't have to, what I'm doing right now, what I'm thinking, and what I will do tomorrow, and he loves me. All of me. He wants to be with me.

I don't get it but I can, little by little, trust him, believe what he says, and trust that he wants me even when my "don't trust anybody..bad things happen when you do" alarms go off.

So what does it look like to let him serve me? I don't know. I really don't. But my heart says..okay I am willing to let him. As scary as it is, I am willing. Show me the way.

How does it feel to hear Jesus say "let me serve you"?

Can you let him?

If not, why not? What's in the way?

8

It's Dead. Or is it? It looks like it, but is it really?

I took a refresher course to maintain my certification in a trauma processing protocol I use in ministry. As the leader was praying, she saw a vision of Jesus on the cross and the word "cost" came to her mind. She didn't know what that meant so she asked God to show us. Nothing came to my mind, but I wondered what it meant for me personally. I thought, "I don't want to take his gift for granted. He paid a high price so that I could walk in freedom and help others to do the same."

On the last morning of training, we all prayed and that vision of the cross came back to my mind with the following thoughts: even Jesus' disciples thought he was dead. Like dead dead. And with that, the death of all their hopes, their dreams, and their future. He was the Messiah, he was going to make everything right, he was going to be the king, but he was dead. What now? I imagine despair set in. They may have been thinking, "This is not what we expected, it's hopeless, it's all over, and what do we do now?" Seems like a bleak situation, but this was NOT death! Everything about it looked like it, but LIFE was coming! It was NOT over! It was just beginning! Life was on the other side.

What I'm experiencing may look like death in the shape of: this is not the marriage I hoped for, my kids have gone in the opposite direction, my health isn't how I wanted it to be, my loved ones are gone and they weren't supposed to be this soon, my friends deserted me when I thought they would walk with me, people I thought were *for* me are spreading false things, or I'm stuck in a wounded place and can't get free.

On the other side of death, life is coming! So what does life look like for me? What things look dead and hopeless? Can I look and hope for life on the other side of it all? What is God up to and where is he in this? What does he want me to let go of, if anything, to embrace the life he has for me?

What about you? How would you answer these questions?

9

Known

"A woman of Samaria came to draw water. 'Give me a drink,' Jesus said to her, because his disciples had gone into town to buy food. 'How is it that you, a Jew, ask for a drink from me, a Samaritan woman?' She asked him. For Jews do not associate with Samaritans." John 4:7-9

Jesus didn't care about the rules. He cared about HER. He saw her. He sees me as I truly am too, not through the filter of what I've done, or what I'm currently doing. He calls out my true identity. He calls me into relationship not into rules.

My profession is caring for people. I see in them what they don't see, and who they really are, not the brokenness they present. Jesus sees that in me. Can I see that in myself? Or do I see myself through the lens of shame?

How do you see you?

Parched

26

10

Parched

A few years ago, I planted a garden for the first time. I planted lots of things, to see what would grow. I tended it every day, until my grandmother passed away in July. She was in the hospital for a couple of weeks before she passed, and I stayed with her as much as I could.

July is one of the hottest months in Oklahoma. I wasn't thinking about watering my garden and everything died. The ground was parched, cracked, hard, and not able to sustain plant life. As I was thinking about the dry earth, I noted the similarity in myself. That's how I felt. Cracked, parched, maybe not hardened yet, but I could become that way if I wasn't mindful of how easily I could.

There is no...how to quench my parched self in three easy steps...plan. That's not how life goes. It takes time, accepting the moment I'm in, allowing grief to be a process, telling the story to friends, sharing the sadness with my family, taking life moment by moment at times, and allowing Jesus to be my comfort in the hard hard moments.

el energized and regain some sense of
nd joy in before, but I'm not there yet.

..ɔ you get through the hard things in life?

11

Change

I heard this on a podcast. I wish I could remember who said it, to give them proper credit, but I don't. However, it's too good not to share!

The quote was, "Even though where I am is painful, to let go and embrace the unknown is sometimes more painful than where I am. If I believe a different story, I have a fear of that story because who would I be without this story of suffering? I have lived in the wrong story so long, I would rather live in a wrong story than endure the fear of losing my identity in the hallway between the room I'm in and the room I'm going toward."

Things to think about. I don't want my identity to be rooted in a wrong story. I'd like to embrace the truth even if it's scary.

Are you living in a wrong story?

Do you want to live in a different one?

Layla and Riley

12

Perspective

I have two dogs, one big and one small, I have a small back yard where they do their business, and on a regular basis-ahem, maybe not so regular if I'm honest, I get to clean up their poo so they have places to poo! Yes, we're really talking about poo!

I walk up one side and back down the other, picking up as I go. On one occasion, I walked up one side and thought I had everything in that space picked up. I was surprised on my way back, that I had missed several piles. I thought about vantage point and perspective.

If I only look through my own filter or lens, I get a partial view of the situation. If I can look at it from a different angle..someone else's view point...I see things I missed when I was only seeing from my perspective.

How about you?

Are there times when you were surprised to become aware of something you hadn't thought of before?

13

What If?

"Now a woman suffering from bleeding for twelve years had endured much under many doctors. She had spent everything she had and was not helped at all. On the contrary, she became worse. Having heard about Jesus, she came up behind him in the crowd and touched his clothing. For she said, 'If I just touch his clothes, I'll be made well.' Instantly her flow of blood ceased, and she sensed in her body that she was healed of her affliction.

Immediately Jesus realized that power had gone out from him. He turned around in the crowd and said, 'Who touched my clothes?'

His disciples said to him, 'You see the crowd pressing against you, and yet you say, who touched me?'

But he was looking around to see who had done this. The woman, with fear and trembling, knowing what had happened to her, came and fell down before him, and told him the whole truth.

'Daughter,' he said to her, 'your faith has saved you. Go in peace and be healed from your affliction.'" Mark 5:25-34.

I want to focus on Jesus asking who touched his clothes. He knew who touched his clothes, yet he asked. Why did he ask?

What if he wanted to heal more than her physical affliction? We are complicated humans. We can be physically, relationally, emotionally, or spiritually broken. What if he wanted to show her and everyone else that she wasn't just healed, she was wanted, accepted, loved, she belonged, and she was worthy of love. What if it was about relationship? What if Jesus wanted to show the religious teachers of the time that their rules were no longer gonna work because he came to show us HIS way...the way of love?

What do you think?

Spring is coming!

34

14

Transitions

Last spring I noticed the trees. Some were blooming while some still looked quite dead, and I thought of transitions. In the spring, the transition from death to life can take a while. It seems to take forever, at least for my ADHD brain! It might seem quicker to you!

First, I see early signs of life, tiny buds on trees and flowers slowly growing until the right time and condition to bloom. I don't see what's happening on the inside, the preparation before winter turns to spring.

Winter seasons in my life seem so long! In the middle of them, I can't see my way out and wonder if spring will ever come, or if I will see the sunshine again.

The outward observation is, nothing is happening. I don't see the transformation on the inside, but healing is happening, new perceptions forming, deeper awareness of life and how I engage with it surfacing, my frozen soul begins to thaw, and anticipation, whether I'm aware of it or not, of spring is building.

I am grateful when spring arrives, and that winter changed me for the better. I still don't like winter. I'm not a fan literally, or figuratively. But, I like spring and I am willing to let the winter do its work to experience the new life spring brings.

How do you engage with the winter seasons in your life?

What are things that help you in the middle of it?

What encourages you to look for spring?

What discouragements are prohibitive of believing that spring will come?

15

Waiting

I am not patient, I don't like waiting, I hate feeling restricted, and I don't like being slowed down. I get irritated when I can't get done what I want to, when I want to, and I don't naturally have self-restraint. (If it's worth doing, it's worth overdoing!).

I know experientially though, if I get in a hurry and throw something together or cut corners just to get it done, I will hate the end result. If I change grocery lines, I can end up waiting longer than I would have. If I hurry and shovel food in my belly on the go instead of sitting down and thoughtfully eating, I will suffer the heartburn, stomach ache, and other consequences later that will slow me down. If I react to situations with explosive anger, or with harsh words, I may feel better in the moment but the damage I leave in the wake, is hard to repair.

So why am I telling you? I am learning and trying to practice having a considered response (pause, think, respond), rather than my default conditioned one (fire, ready, aim!). It's a daily process. Sometimes I fail more than I succeed and sometimes I succeed more than I fail. I'm a work in progress.

Do you struggle in waiting?

If not, what are things you do struggle with?

16

Under The Surface

As I was trying my luck with gardening a couple of years ago, I was learning that certain plants don't like each other, and others do, some like full sun and others like shade, some need space and others need cover, some need more water and others need less water, some like alkaline soil and others like acidic soil, and the list goes on. There's so much to know about plants and their living conditions!

Water is important and I wanted to make sure I got that right, so I watered every single day. I went out in the morning or late afternoon and looked at the ground to see if it was moist or dry. Most of the time it looked dry so I watered it. Then I noticed the leaves on my plants doing strange things. What was going on?!

To find out, I bought a handy dandy soil moisture meter. Oh my goodness! The ground underneath the top layer was saturated. I was literally drowning my plants and had no idea. It looked dry on the top!

People are like that. They present a certain way on the outside but that's not who they are underneath. I'm thinking of it in a negative context but I guess it could go either way. Some people can look really friendly on the outside and be treacherous underneath. I've encountered a few of them. I hope I haven't ever been one of them!

I want to look beyond what's outwardly apparent, and look deeper into what's someone's story? What happened in a life that led to this point? Who is the amazing person under the armor? My own brokenness gets in the way sometimes but that's who I want to be. I'm working on it.

How about you?

Who do you want to be?

What do you struggle with that keeps you from being who you want to be?

17

Over There

My husband and I were gifted a weekend at the lake in an RV. The site was pretty, had trees, not many people, and was close to the water. The weather was nice. It was a perfect day.

Across the water was another camp site. From where I stood, it looked really pretty. Later that day, we walked around our campsite and over to the other campsite. When we got there, I realized it wasn't as nice as where we were.

I was reminded that just because something looks better than what I have, it doesn't mean it is. What if what I have has been especially tailored for me and other things won't fit because they weren't made for me? They were made for someone else.

I came home from the weekend feeling content and thankful. I'm happy with the things I have. That doesn't mean I don't want more, but I'm not dissatisfied with what I have.

Are you content with what you have? Or do you find yourself wishing you had something different? If so, do you judge yourself harshly? Can you accept that in the moment, this is true about you, love yourself anyway and move on? I hope you choose the latter!

1970's Dining Chair

18

Upholstery Business

I was working on recovering and repairing a dining room chair my grandparents had when I was growing up. The chair had been exposed to rain and all kinds of weather so the wood had rotted, the frame had some rust on it, and the foam and the vinyl (it was olive green vinyl from the 1970's) needed to be replaced.

I wanted to preserve as much of the shape of the wood as I could in order to construct a new piece, so I carefully removed the staples from the bottom of the seat to not damage what was left.

I thought about how God is with me. He doesn't just rip off and throw away the areas in my heart that need healing, or ways of thinking that won't serve me well. He gingerly leads me with a kind and gentle hand, carefully and tenderly removing the old broken things, preserving what's healthy, and making things new so I can experience healing and growth.

Have you ever felt like you were being reupholstered? If so, how was it for you?

If you attribute it to God, do you see him as kind and loving, or harsh and angry? Why or why not?

44

19

Push or Quit?

In the last story, I told you about a chair I was repairing. It was a pretty big undertaking and once I get focused and start working, I don't want to quit. I had drawn an outline on wood, to cut with the jig saw. As I was working, dusk was approaching. I didn't want to quit but it was getting harder to see the line. And, I was using a power tool! I had a choice. Press on, trying to guess where to cut, or pack it in for the night. I reluctantly called it a day, put up my tools, and left the rest for the next day.

Sounds simple. Of course I'd go inside when it's dark; however, that's not how I'm wired. I hyper-focus and I'm time blind, functions of the ADHD.

I'm not aware of the passage of time or how long it will take me to complete something. I wanted to keep pushing, "just to get this last thing done". Only that last thing leads to another and another.

A teeny little voice inside my brain said, "self, if you continue, you will create more work for yourself tomorrow and it will take longer to fix what you messed up tonight." I listened to that voice and saved myself a considerable amount of trouble.

The next day, I felt rested, I could see clearly, and I finished my task. I'm glad I waited. I don't always and I generally wish I did!

Do you have similar experiences?

If so, what are they like?

Do you push ahead and regret it? Or do you heed the nudge to quit?

How do you feel afterward?

20

Impatient

I had been working on a project that was taking longer than I wanted it to. I'm impatient. I enjoy the process of working on things but I also get tired and want them to be done.

This was one of those days. I thought I was done, put up all my supplies, and on closer inspection, realized I missed some things. I was tired andI didn't want to get all the stuff back out. I was tempted to cut corners and try and hide it with some creative maneuvers. I knew though, if I did, I wouldn't be happy with my work.

So when I'm tired and frustrated, what do I do? Do I give up and quit? Throw my hands up and say "I can't do this"? Cut corners? If I do, can mistakes be okay? When I'm stuck can I ask for help? Or will I be determined to do it myself and miss an opportunity to be cared for? Will I still be loved even in my weakness?

These are questions I wrestle through just about every day and I need to answer them because they are important. How I answer them will decide how I perceive myself on any given day.

How will you answer these questions?

Do you like the answers you come up with?

Do your answers help you to like who you are, or do they condemn you?

21

Dream

Years ago, I had the same dream on three consecutive nights. The context of each dream was something very familiar, something routine, but in each dream something was very out of place that didn't belong in the context of the dream.

After the third night, I started asking God what the dreams meant. I generally have to have something brought to my attention three times before I actually take notice. Ha. Anyhow, I asked what they meant.

The answer was, "You cannot discern what's true with your natural senses. You must seek me for truth."

What does that mean? There are things that look normal, unremarkable, good, but I can't count on what I perceive, to represent truth. Conversely, things can look really bad but might not be. I need to ask God what the truth is and let him show me.

Do you get locked in to your perceptions of what's true?
Or do you challenge them to find out what's actually true?
If you follow Jesus, do you trust Him to show you?

Frame

22

Frame

When we moved into the house we live in now, the door between the kitchen and laundry room had a small cat/dog door in it, with a lockable flap. At the time, I had a little Silky Terrier (she passed away a few years ago). We didn't have the yard fenced yet and I needed the back door open to be able to get a dog (someone else's that I was caring for) into the car to take to the vet. To keep her safe, I put her in the laundry room until I came back. When I returned home, she had chewed all the way around that little opening trying to get out.

I left it that way for a time trying to decide if I wanted to replace the door, or try and salvage the animal opening somehow. I decided to frame it. I cut around the jagged areas, and cut a piece of wood in sections to frame it like a picture frame. I have a dog now who is quite a bit bigger and the expanded hole was big enough for him to fit through and it's nice to have a way to separate the little dog and the cat from the big dog sometimes.

To cut the stick of wood, I used a miter box with a hand saw. I must have moved my hand slightly while I was making the cuts on each piece, and the corners of my frame didn't exactly match. Uh oh! I had a problem.

What was I to do? Scrap the whole thing? Tell it how bad it is for not lining up? Shame myself for not getting it right?, or ask myself, "What now?" What are some options I have?

I can use glue or construction adhesive to affix it to the door and figure out what to do with the mismatch, I can try and staple the frame together, I can sand the corners, I can file it, I can cut it again...there are lots of options.

I decided to glue the frame together at the points that lined up, mount it onto the door, and then use wood filler to fill in the gaps and paint it. That was a splendid idea. I like the way it looks. You wouldn't ever know the condition of it before.

This may seem like a silly example...who would tell sticks of wood they're bad for not lining up and being perfect! With something external, like a project, I can look at it and figure out a way to make it work most of the time.

Here's the thing though, without thinking, I sometimes do that to myself. I am sooo much more valuable and yet, I can still shame myself for not measuring up to the standard I set for myself, or that others place upon me.

If I make a mistake, am I worthless? Of course not! It's just a mistake and mistakes can be worked with. It's not about who I am.

What about you?

Is it okay to not be perfect?

To not measure up?

Are you still valuable?

Are you still worthy of love?

If the answer is no, then why not?

23

Gift

One Sunday at church, I noticed a lady across from me sitting alone, crying. I wondered why my attention was drawn to her. When worship was over, I felt drawn to say to her, "God sees you."

Oh boy. I didn't want to. I experienced something profoundly painful regarding a prophetic gift and I walked away from it, turned my back on it, and said no thank you. I said to God, "If you want someone to know something then you tell them because I'm not going to", and that's where I pitched my tent. Until now.

Reluctantly, I went to this lady and told her what I heard, and she told me the reason for her tears. I listened, just sitting with her in her pain, until it was time for the teaching.

I walked away feeling grateful. I guess I allowed God to soften my heart and heal some of my hurts along the way. In that moment, he saw her, and he also saw me.

I still am hesitant sometimes, but not resistant, to share things I feel invited to share, and am learning to be at peace with the gift I have. I trust that he will continue to heal the places where I hurt.

Are there things you've been given to do that you've walked away from? It doesn't have to be something spiritual.

Is there something you could give yourself permission to return to?

Color

24

Colors

My house is amazing. It was built in 1969 and the previous owners did a crazy amount of work to update it. It was like it had been done just for us, it was that well suited to our taste.

After we had lived here for a year or two, I started noticing that the paint color in the entryway and the hallway seemed harsh. I'm not sure what color you'd call it...there are so many now..let's just call it light brown with yellow undertones.

I am sensitive to how a space feels. Maybe part of the ADHD sensory issues..who knows. If warm colors are combined with cool colors in a space, or if a color seems "loud" it bothers my brain...physically.

So, I decided to paint the hallway a "smoother" color... less harsh in my eyes. Now THAT, was an exercise in frustration. There were so many colors to choose from, I couldn't land on one. I'd find a color card for one I liked at the paint store, then get it home and hate it.

Colors look different in different lighting, in different spaces, on a phone screen, on bigger surfaces, and on smaller surfaces. Different undertones emerge in different lighting and next to other colors. So, what I thought I liked changed based on where it was and how it was placed.

Isn't life like that? I see things in a certain way with a certain perspective based on outward appearances. What I don't know though, is in any given circumstance, there are different undertones, different ways of seeing. There's no way for me to know the true color because the lens I view life through is not a complete picture.

Most colors are mixtures of other colors. The same is true with the things I experience. There's more than one way to look at it.

"For now we see but a faint reflection of riddles and mysteries as though reflected in a mirror, but one day we will see face-to-face. My understanding is incomplete now, but one day I will understand everything, just as everything about me has been fully understood." 1 Corinthians 13:12.

What frustrates you?

Can you recall experiences in which you thought something was one way, then found out it was different?

How did you respond?

25

ANTS

*Once upon a time...*just kidding :) I was showering one
morning and noticed mold growing on the ceiling. I hadn't
noticed it before, but it had been there for a while because
it was now spreading. I had planned on repainting the
bathroom the same color, just a fresh coat. I hadn't
planned on dealing with mold and repainting the ceiling
first.

Ceiling painting is hard for me. I have some
osteoarthritis in my neck and a bit of disc compression that
happens as we age. Looking up and reaching over my head
for extended periods of time is painful. I try to avoid it if I
can.

However, the ceiling had to be attended to. Why?
Because left unaddressed, mold will continue to spread on
the surface and as it spreads, it will grow deeper into the
dry wall. It will eventually take over, not to mention make
you sick. So, I did it. I bought mold killing primer and
ceiling paint and got the job done.

As I worked, I thought about limiting beliefs—
something I believe about myself that restricts me from
moving forward or being who I want to be. I generally am
not aware of them until one gets triggered! Then I become
aware of how long it's been there and how it's affecting me.

If I leave that belief unchallenged, it will consume me and take me in a different direction than I want to go.

Wouldn't it be awesome if there was "limiting belief killing primer" and we could paint over it? I digress. ADHD remember?!

I use a strategy I learned from Dr. Daniel Amen, he calls the ANT killer (ANT-Automatic Negative Thoughts) to challenge those beliefs. I ask myself, is it true? If so, can I absolutely 100% know that it's true? How do I feel when I have this thought? Who would I be without the belief? Turn the belief around, is the turn around true, or even truer than the original belief?

It looks like this: Say my belief is, I can't do anything right. **Is that true?** Seems like it. **Can I absolutely 100% know that it's true?** Well no, since you put it that way. **How do I feel when I believe I can't do anything right?** Sad, frustrated, discouraged. **Who would I be without believing I can't do anything right?** I'd be energized to try more things. **Turning the belief around:** I do lots of things right. Sometimes I mess up but that's part of learning and growing. **Is the turn around true or even truer than the original belief?** Yes. Absolutely.

Do you have ANTS? I bet ya do. Try this out. Go kill some ANTS. :)

26

Weeds

In the spring and summer months, I spend as much time as I can outdoors, observing things in nature. Being outside is my happy place. I can think more clearly, for some reason, when I'm digging in dirt or just being outside in general.

A couple of summers ago, I was in my garden pulling weeds and trying not to pull up the tender little plants that had just started growing. I noticed that some of those weeds had roots that went on forever. Well..maybe not forever, but they go way deep and their root system is strong. It's really hard to pull them out. Many of them break off and I don't get the root. They seem to grow without attention. They have to be sturdy I guess, to withstand nature.

Plants, on the other hand, are delicate and require tender care. Except for carrots. :) Plants can be easily traumatized and their delicate root system damaged. Some plants are hardier, but I'm talking about the tender ones. If I let the weeds grow, they will crowd out the plants. Weeds seem to take over and own the whole garden.

My internal landscape is kind of like that. There are tender plants...my healing, coming into awareness of my true identity, learning to recognize limiting beliefs, self acceptance, learning healthy ways to do life, overcoming negative self talk, and all the good things there are for me. Then there are the weeds...negative thoughts and beliefs, self criticism, self-condemnation, unhealthy patterns, being hard on myself, and every other negative temptation out there.

I won't be getting rid of all the weeds for all time. I sure wish I could! They exist just like the weeds in nature, and some are even beneficial to help me grow. The toxic weeds can be hard to uproot, but if I let them go untended they will take over and smother the plants. That's not what I want!

The good news is, I can actually change the grooves in my brain over time, by thinking new thoughts and challenging the old. The term is neuroplasticity.

Wikipedia defines neuroplasticity as "the ability of neural networks in the brain to change through growth and reorganization. It is when the brain is rewired to function in some way that differs from how it previously functioned."

Verywellmind.com defines it as "the brain's ability to change, reorganize, or grow neural networks. Plasticity refers to the brain's malleability or ability to change. Neuro refers to neurons, the nerve cells that are the building blocks of the brain and nervous system. Thus, neuroplasticity allows nerve cells to change or adjust."

It was once thought that the brain's ability to grow new neurons stopped right after birth. That is not the consensus today. If you're curious and want to know more, do some research into neuroplasticity. Fascinating stuff!

How about you? What are your weeds? What are your plants?

How will you nurture the plants?

Does it bring you hope to think that you can change your brain and learn new patterns of thinking? Why or why not?

St Louis Bridge

27

Bridge

Have you ever driven over a river bridge? I have. It's quite an experience. I'm not talking about a small body of water. I'm talking about an expansive one. All I could see under me was water. Everywhere. There was nothing between me and that water...except the bridge. As I drove over that water though, I fully expected that what was under me would hold me up. I trusted that the foundation was sturdy and that the builders took great care in making sure it was.

Do I have that same trust in life? Do I trust that I will be supported, that what's under me is sturdy, that I will get to the other side without drowning? Do I trust the builder of my foundation (for me, Jesus) to carry me?

What about you? What holds you up?

Do you trust your foundation? If so, why? And if not, why not?

28

Can I have a dog?

I've always loved dogs. There was only a very short time in my life when I didn't have one.

In 2017 I lost my best dog. That was so very hard, and the next year I lost my other dog. After that, I thought I'd try not having a dog. I thought of all the things I could do without the responsibility, thought of the money I'd save, all the yard cleanups I wouldn't have to do, and....I made it three months without a dog. I missed them greeting me at the door when I got home, all the snuggles, and the companionship.

So I started researching. I had a list of things I wanted. I wanted a dog that didn't shed, or bark much, that liked people, other dogs, kids, and cats (I have a cat), was a medium sized dog, and one I could train to be a therapy dog to help with traumatized clients. It would be a miracle if I found one that checked off all the things. Guess what?! I found one.

I decided on a Havanese, and then looked at how much they cost. There wasn't any way I could afford it. Literally no way. For some reason I kept looking though, checking classified ads, Craigs list, pet finder, AKC...anywhere I could search and I found a few puppy scams along the way. Grrr!

Months went buy and I was getting discouraged. How could something so perfect be impossible to get? I was about to give up and out of exasperation more than anything, said with a big sigh, "God, can I have a dog?" I hadn't asked before. I'm not sure why. Maybe I thought it wasn't worth him caring about. And to be honest, I really didn't expect to find one.

The next day, I was searching the newspaper classified ads and there before my very eyes, was an ad for a Havanese from a local breeder. I had JUST searched that same paper the day before. I thought this surely must be a scam, but I called the number anyway. Nope, not a scam. A real person with real dogs answered the phone. The dog parents were on site and I could come see them, look at the puppies, ask questions, and get whatever information I needed.

The breeder's place was a couple of hours from where I live, so off I went. There's a back story to this.

In 2014, I had a wreck that totaled my car..badly. I received insurance money to cover the medical treatment I needed and the insurance company let me "buy back" the wrecked car. It sat in my garage until I finally placed an ad to sell the motor in it. It had survived somehow. In a short while, someone who was restoring another mustang bought the car from us. I put the money away so it wouldn't just get spent.

Back to the dog story. I went to look at the puppies. Everything was just as the breeder had represented and as I was talking with the her, I found out she was a therapist (I'm a counselor) and wanted to train therapy dogs also. Unbelievable. There's more. The amount of money I had in my pocket from the sale of the car was the amount of money she asked for the puppy. Of course, I bought the puppy. He was perfect.

I walked away from that experience with my jaw on the floor almost. God saw me and he cared. He cared that I wanted a dog. He was just waiting for me to ask. I picture him like a dad who knows his child longs for something. He wants so badly to to give the gift, and he's just waiting for his child to ask. Can you just feel the anticipation, and the love of Jesus? I can.

Are there things you are afraid to ask for?

What's stopping you?

Hidden

29

Hidden

I was shampooing my living room rug one day after a little umm dog mishap! The rug is white and I went over that rug at least 5 times to get it cleaned. When I was satisfied that I had cleaned the heck out of it, I thought...ya know...I probably should look at the bottom just to make sure. The bottom was NOT clean. Gross. So I flipped the rug over and made at least five passes on that side with the shampooer.

So what's my point? In our culture, I've been trained to suck it up, put on a smile, move on, and never let anything show, but what's underneath? Am I addressing what's there? Because, if I don't, I will not be able to be all that I was designed to be or what I could be.

Believe me, the last thing I want to do is look weak or be vulnerable, but is it worth it? The cost of being hidden and not allowing what's underneath to be seen is high. Let's change this together.

Are you in?

30

New

As I was pulling up dead plants in my garden one day, I was thinking dead things have to be dealt with before new things can live. Without removing the old, the new won't thrive. If old plants were infected, disease could be passed to new plants, dead things take up space preventing living things from growing, dead plants can rob new plants of nutrients they need, and more. I am a very novice gardener so you pro's out there, humor me!

As I considered the plants, I thought about life. If I hold on to unhealthy thinking patterns, I won't experience healing that comes from new ways of thinking. If I hold on to old hurts, I won't experience joy in the good things. If I hold on to something when it's time to let it go, I won't experience the rewards of what I'm being drawn to.

I am in that process now, letting go of something to embrace a new path. It's not easy and I have mixed emotions...excitement, terror and sadness that this is really happening. All at the same time. Yet, I'm compelled to move forward, embracing the feelings that come with letting go, and trusting that better things are ahead than I can even imagine!

Are you currently in, or have you been, in a place of letting go?

How is/was that for you?

Storms

31

Storms

All of us HAVE walked through, ARE walking through, or WILL walk through storms. No one escapes them. As with stormy weather, they're just part of life.

I was on a missions trip to Alabama recently and we had some down time to enjoy the beach. It was raining this day and from the deck, I was watching the waves of the ocean with the rain. I noticed birds on top of the water, not flying in the storm but not going under either. Just sitting there. Waiting. They were built to be buoyant on the water. And so they sat. I've seen other days when birds keep flying even though it's difficult in the wind and rain.

When I face storms, most of the time I want to just push through and try to forget what's happening. I am not a fan of waiting. I don't like it one bit. You know though....there is a time to push through, and there is a time to wait. The tricky part is knowing the difference and trusting that if it is time to wait, I will be carried and sustained. I will not drown. Growth and healing happen in the waiting just as they do in the pushing through.

When you encounter storms, what's your go-to?

Conclusion

I hope you've been intrigued, challenged, encouraged, inspired, given hope, and I hope you've had some laughs as you've walked through a snap shot of my life with me.

Many of the stories have been presented through a christian worldview because that's my life. It doesn't matter where you are, or what you believe, I think you can find something relatable even if you don't agree with my conclusions. We all share the same struggles in life and it's okay see things differently.

There will be more "Odds and Ends" to come at a later date. Until then, I'm with you, I'm for you, I have confidence in you, and you've got this!!